THE
STUDY
OF
LIVING LANGUAGES

THE STUDY OF LIVING LANGUAGES

SIR ARTHUR COTTON

GYAN

Published by

GYAN

Gyan Publishing House
5, Ansari Road
Daryaganj, New Delhi-110002
Phone: 011-47034999, 9811692060
E-mail: books@gyanbooks.com

Distribution Network
gyanbooks.com
India, USA, Canada, UK, Australia

ISBN: 978-93-7014-491-0 (HB)

First Published, 1857

2nd Impression 2025

Printed at: Gyan Press, Delhi.

THE STUDY OF LIVING LANGUAGES
Author: SIR ARTHUR COTTON

THE STUDY OF LIVING LANGUAGES.

BY

COLONEL ARTHUR COTTON,

MADRAS ENGINEERS.

MADRAS:

PRINTED AND PUBLISHED AT THE SCOTTISH PRESS,

BY L. C. GRAVES.

1857.

PREFACE.

The learning of the living languages of foreign, semi-civilized, and savage people has now become a matter of such immeasurable importance that any man may be excused who makes the poorest attempt to diminish the difficulties of such a work.

Englishmen especially, are at this moment employed by thousands, as Merchants, Missionaries, Magistrates, &c., in learning hundreds of different languages spoken by people in all stages of civilization, from the lowest state of society upwards, and in their speedy acquisition of a correct knowledge and free colloquial use of several tongues of those tribes, hundreds of millions of the human race are most deeply interested, as that upon which mainly depends both their temporal and eternal interests. Yet I am not aware that there is in existence a single work in which this subject is closely and systematically investigated. It must be observed that the point before us is, what is the best mode of acquiring a knowledge of the language of savage and semi-civilized nations? and that this is in some important respects quite distinct from both the acquisition of dead languages and also of the living languages of nations who have been fully civilized and, consequently, have a complete system of literature, a great variety of books of instruction written by extensively informed Natives, and also thoroughly educated teachers.

There are difficulties in learning the languages of semi-civilized and barbarous people which do not exist in the case of the languages of civilized nations, and with respect to the dead languages the principal points to be attended to and the objects aimed at are so entirely different from those in living languages, that what is applicable to the one is almost entirely inapplicable to the other.

Nothing can be more deplorable than this state of things. The mischiefs arising out of it are incalculable. All, without exception who require to know such a language, and who make attempts to acquire it, lose, probably from three fourths, to nineteen twentieths of the time so employed; a large portion lose the whole, breaking down before they have acquired any useful knowledge at all; probably scarcely one in ten acquires a tolerably correct and free use of it, and scarcely one at all such a knowledge as to make them really effective translators, an office of the highest possible importance, because the transference of English literature, for the great mass of the inhabitants of the earth, must precede the formation of a national literature among each tribe.

At present it may safely be said that no system whatever is followed in studying such living languages for colloquial purposes. Let any one individual of the thousands who are at this moment so employed, be asked, whose system of study do you prefer, or have you any of your own, and upon what grounds do you decide upon this, or that point, and his answer would generally be such as to show that he had no clear, definite, well-digested ideas on the subject. Without the least previous investigation of the subject, without spending one single day in reading a treatise on it, or considering it in his own mind, he usually blindly takes in hand a matter upon which he will perhaps employ one or several years; taking at a venture as it were, any books or teachers that he may happen to fall in with, or any ideas he may happen to have got into his own head, he knows not how or whence; without any solid grounds for concluding whether the mode he is pursuing will lead to an economical or an enormously wasteful expenditure of time, and, what is of more importance, whether he is laying the foundation of a real, correct, and effective knowledge of the language, or establishing himself in a totally false use of it, which, when become habitual, will never be corrected.

Matters are in respect of this study of languages just as they were in respect of road making before the time of Mr. McAdam. Every man thought he was born a road maker, and those holding the charge of roads did almost anything to them and called it repairs. It was a most common thing for instance to throw a thick layer of loose rounded gravel on the road, which at first caused almost the greatest possible resistance to the carriages and by degrees was converted into mud, but never afforded any thing approaching to a clean, hard surface. The road menders were quite satisfied because they were doing something, but if asked, why they did what produced an effect exactly the opposite to that which was desired, they of course could not have given a reason. Road-making has since been thoroughly investigated and though men have not yet perhaps found out the best way of doing it, they have now a real reason for what they do, and consequently a prodigious improvement in roads has been produced.

It is high time that such a change should take place in reference to this subject now before us, and any attempt at an examination of it, with a view to a really sound system of study should be accepted.

The thoughts contained in the following paper are the results of such a consideration of the subject as could be given to it in the midst of duties of another kind during a period of more than thirty years.

Circumstances have not allowed of the writer following up the study of any language, to any extent, having repeatedly moved, from where one language was spoken to where another was used, and his time being too much occupied with pressing business; nor has he had an opportunity of commencing the study of a language with such materials as he here recommends ready prepared to his hands.

In the course of this long period however he has had an opportunity of trying his plans partially in several languages both on himself and others, and thus of correcting in some measure his first ideas and forming something like a digested system in his own mind; and he must state that as to the leading points in the system here proposed, he has quite satisfied himself.

He has taken every opportunity of obtaining aid from others, both by reading works of teachers of languages in Europe, and also by trying to discuss the question with those who were studying and had studied such kind of living languages. From the former he has received some help, though often merely by being taught what to avoid; but from the latter he received no assistance, simply because in general they had no distinct ideas at all on the matter, nor any solid reason for any thing they had done in their studies. He has however got various hints from observing what progress different men had made in such studies when using different means. On one occasion he met with a young man who had given his whole time to Arabic for three years, and could not then produce a sentence in conversation, and soon after he was intimate with another who in about 8 months and while loaded with other duties, had obtained, if not an accurate yet such an *effective,* colloquial use of the same tongue, that he regularly transacted extensive business in it with strangers of all sorts without the least difficulty. Again, in India one meets every day with men who have studied most diligently for one, two or three years, and yet all their life after speak a language, that both from pronunciation and expression is almost, or quite, unintelligible to any native, excepting those who from being about them constantly in an official capacity have *learnt their* language, (for what they used and called the native language was really a language of their own invention) and so have come to understand them.

The writer cannot conclude these remarks without expressing his full assurance that the acquisition of a correct knowledge and perfectly ready colloquial use of such languages will be found to be a matter requiring very little time compared with what it does at present, in most cases, when a better mode of learning is adopted. On one occasion he had an opportunity of observing the progress made by children in acquiring a new language in a certain time. Out of a number that embarked in a ship in India many did not know a word of English, having previously used nothing but some Indian language, and they were of various ages. During the four months of the voyage to England every one of them had so perfectly acquired the use of English that they never were at a loss, and latterly seemed to have as good a knowledge of it as those who had always used it. Now if children of a few years old, without the slightest assistance from teachers or study, could thus pick up a colloquial use of a new language in four months and talk it exactly like one who had never talked any thing else, it seems certain that adults with a hundred times their power of mind and with suitable books and teachers and regular study could not fail to attain to a real knowledge and ready colloquial use of a new language, and that without being years about it, unless they were altogether wrong in the method of study they adopted. In fact he cannot help declaring it as his opinion that when this subject is fairly grappled with by men, the great supposed obstacles to intercourse of strange languages will be found, comparatively speaking, a mere bugbear ; and that the acquisition of a new language for all the ordinary purposes of life will be found to be within the reach of almost all with a comparatively very small expenditure of time and labour.

THE STUDY

OF

LIVING LANGUAGES.

Before proceeding to propose a system of study of living languages, it may be well to make some remarks on the mistakes that are commonly made at present, and the chief difficulties that are usually met with, as well as on the time generally expended on such study.

A great many of the common mistakes can easily be traced to the circumstance that almost universally the students have previously been accustomed to study dead languages, and from their not observing that almost all their ideas have been formed from *that* study, while the principal points to be attended to in the study of living languages are exactly those that are of little or no consequence in that of dead ones, and *vice versâ*. In learning Latin or Greek, for instance, the sole objects usually are to be able to read so as to understand the writings of highly educated men and (but as very secondary) to write elegant formal essays. The following are therefore the leading points aimed at;

1st. A knowledge of the character.

2nd. A knowledge of the whole vocabulary of the language, including a multitude of words seldom or never used colloquially in the ordinary business of life.

3rd. A readiness in perceiving the meaning of long involved formal sentences, such as are found in grave prose and in poetical writings.

4th. A thorough knowledge of the whole grammar, so as to be able to give a formal rule for any thing when questioned.

5th. And such a familiar knowledge of the idiom of the language as will enable one to write formal papers in a good style.

The points that are of little or no consequence are,

1st. Correct pronunciation.

2nd. An extensive knowledge of the common expressions used in the ordinary business of life.

3rd. A perfect readiness at recognizing the word by the sound when rapidly spoken.

4th. The same in forming sentences to express our own thoughts.

Now, if we consider these things we shall perceive that the study of the dead languages and that of the living languages of semi-civilized and barbarous nations are almost diametrically opposed in respect of the objects to be attained. The points that are essential in the one are either non-essential, or of no importance whatever, in the other and *vice versa.* A man may talk a language most fluently, correctly and usefully, for all the ordinary business of life, without knowing the character, without being able to quote a single rule of grammar, without the knowledge of half or three-fourths of the vocabulary of a language, and without any facility in comprehending the involved sentences of formal writings of learned men ; while, without an accurate pronunciation, an ample acquaintance with the common colloquial expressions of uneducated people, and a most free and ready use of them, so that strangers can readily catch his words and comprehend his meaning, and without an ear thoroughly exercised in the sounds of the language, so as at once to recognise what is spoken by a native, he has entirely missed his object, though he may know every word in the language and every rule of grammar, and be able to write an elegant essay without a mistake. Books of history &c. do not furnish us with the expressions of ordinary conversation. *Every country has its own peculiar forms and they must be learnt individually* ; no rules can be given by which a student, who knows the words and grammar, can invent them himself. In semi-civilized countries, where not one in a hundred has read books, there is a large proportion of the words, which are never used in conversation on ordinary matters, and which therefore are so far from being of any use to the great mass of those who have to acquire the language that they are always in his way, if he has learnt them, leading him to express himself in words not in common use, and consequently unknown to most of those with whom he has to communicate. So far therefore from it being sufficient to follow the ideas which a man has gathered while studying dead languages, they are in fact the very opposite to those which are correct as respects the study of such living languages as are here supposed.

If we examine the mode of study adopted generally, however it may vary in minor points, the system, so far as that can be called a system, which is indeed no such thing, is that suited to the dead languages. A man takes up a book of stories, a grammar, and a dictionary, and learning, almost exclusively by the eye, he proceeds exactly as if the use of his ear were of no consequence, as if he must at once grapple with the whole vocabulary of the language, and as if when he had got the materials of words and rules of grammar, he could himself guess the forms of expression which he must compound from them; like the idiot who was found to have stored up in his box all the wheels, axles, &c., he could lay his hand upon, thinking that when he had got enough he could easily make a clock of them. The results of this proceeding are notorious. A youth in India has passed a splendid examination, knows every word of the language and has a rule of grammar for everything, loses his way out riding and can't get home before he is in danger of a stroke of the sun, because he can't make any Native he meets understand him, nor can he understand a sentence spoken by them, and this after many months, often a year or two, of intense study from morning to night. And what is still worse, probably he is confirmed in a false pronunciation and a false mode of expression from having almost entirely neglected these two great essentials, or at least not having given them any thing like due attention. The consideration of this source of many of the most serious mistakes that are made in this study will be very useful.

Another great source of mistakes, is that such languages are generally learnt by men at that age when they have most confidence in their own powers and when they are consequently always disposed to take the bull by the horns. With this feeling the student generally rushes into the midst of his enemies headlong, attempting to grapple at once with the character, the pronunciation, the whole grammar, the whole vocabulary of 20,000, or, as in Arabic, 200,000 words, the language of books and the language of conversation &c. No wonder that such a one finds himself continually discouraged, that many give up in despair, that all waste an enormous amount of time and mental effort, and that scarcely one in a hundred ever talks like a native. Whatever a man's powers may be it is certainly sheer waste to set about matters in this way, and he cannot possibly receive such clear impressions on his mind as the same person would, if he concentrated his attention upon one thing at a time.

It may also be well here to advert to some peculiar difficulties which we necessarily encounter in the circumstances in which Europeans are ordinarily placed in semi-civilized countries, and especially in a country like India, in which caste prevails. If an Englishman wishes to learn French or German, he can go and live with a native family, or throw himself continually into the society of natives, in inns and places of public resort, where his ear will be exercised from morning to night in the true pronunciation and the real ordinary expressions of the language, and where consequently, without the least effort even, though indeed slowly, he can hardly help acquiring a correct use of the language both as respects pronunciation and expression. But there are few countries out of Europe where a European can thus freely associate with the natives, and in India he is effectually excluded from their houses. Separate and special means must therefore be used, to exercise the tongue and ear of the student, and to store his memory with a stock of bona fide expressions.

Another difficulty is the great inferiority of native teachers compared with European Masters. Indeed in a great proportion of cases a man has to learn a language with the assistance of one who is not a teacher at all by profession, and who therefore cannot give him a hundredth part of the help derived from a practised and well instructed teacher. Further, such languages are so extremely different from the European tongues, in every respect that a person is much more likely to be discouraged from the difficulties he experiences than in learning a foreign European language, and on this account it is especially necessary to adopt a system that shall as far as possible tend to *keep up the student's courage.*

These are some of the leading points that should be kept in view in considering a system of study for such languages.

I would now propose some fundamental principles to be taken as clues to the better understanding of the subject.

It is evident that there are two fundamental points to be attended to. The first, which is by far of the greatest importance of the two, is; To be careful that we lay a sound foundation. This is a universal principle and yet one at least as often forgotten in studying languages as in other matters. If a false foundation is laid, the erection can never be made sound. If a man once acquires a false pronunciation or a false mode of expression, he will never get over it. Whatever he learns should be perfectly correct, and not only so, he should have such a thorough knowledge of it that he shall be fully assured in his own mind that his knowledge is correct, so that he may not afterwards be in doubt and liable to give up what is right and substitute some guess of his own instead. For want of right modes of study, what numbers use all their lives some language and pronunciation of their own invention and never find out how it is they can hardly have any intercourse with natives by means of it. The true *value* and true pronunciation of every word encountered should be fully ascertained, and its use in a great variety of forms of expression should be made thoroughly familiar, before proceeding to other words, and no imperfect acquaintance with a word or expression should be allowed. The second great principle is of course; To save time; but this must always be subordinate to the former. In the main however the two principles are not only compatible but inseparable: nothing causes so much waste of time as imperfectly learning things, receiving indistinct and shallow impressions of them, because such things are always forgotten and have to be learnt over again. This is the grand reason why such enormous time is wasted in this study. A man attempts so much at once that every thing is partially learnt and forgotten probably at least a hundred times over. He begins with a book containing hundreds, more likely thousands of words and long sentences involving innumerable rules of grammar, and before he gets to the end of it has learnt in a sort of way and forgotten every word in it and every expression over and over again, and has probably in the end thoroughly apprehended and acquired a familiar knowledge of not one twentieth part of the words he has met with. He perhaps makes lists of the words that he meets with and learns many hundreds by heart at once, but he has no useful knowledge of one in twenty of them. No word is effectually known till it is so thoroughly familiar, that it is ready in his mouth at any moment, without the slightest effort of memory, and till it can be used in a considerable variety of expressions; in fact, till it is just to the student like one of the words of his native tongue, and so wrought into his mind that it cannot be forgotten again. It may however often appear that time would be gained by adopting some plan which would endanger the soundness of the foundation, and in this case such a plan must be rejected.

The third great principle is; To have such a system as shall encourage people, both to commence upon and go through with the study of native languages. It is of exceeding importance to encourage all persons, whatever their situations or occupations are, when remaining for any time however short or uncertain in such countries, to make themselves acquainted, as far as possible, with the language of the people. Numbers at present never attempt it, solely because the usual mode of study cuts them off from all hope of ever attaining to the smallest useful knowledge of it, without such an expenditure of time and labour as they are afraid to encounter or their circumstances absolutely prevent. A system which shall afford some useful results to every one who enters upon it, and those in some degree proportioned to the time and labour expended, is an immense desideratum. It would lead numbers to make a beginning who now never attempt it; and many such, if they once began, would not rest till they had obtained some considerable knowledge of it.

An encouraging system is equally required for those who do at present set themselves to the study with the purpose of going through with it. Nothing can be more discouraging than the means usually pursued at present, whereas if a man were pursuing a system in which he felt at every step, that he was making real, useful progress, he would go on with tenfold spirit, always feeling too, that stop where he would, his labour had not been thrown away.

In endeavouring to accomplish the first object the following rules may be laid down.

1st. The student is really to *learn* the language and not to attempt to *teach himself*. For instance, nothing is more common than for a man, as soon as he has learnt a few words, with the help of his grammar to begin to try and form sentences. In this way he may certainly make a new language of his own, but it won't be the language he proposes to learn. Thus numbers attempt to communicate with Natives by English sentences made up of foreign words which consequently are not merely scarcely intelligible but often convey no meaning at all, though perfectly correct as regards both words and grammar. The student must not at first attempt to take the smallest step alone. He must not pronounce a word nor put two words together by himself. He must be content to *learn* every thing, and that thoroughly, from a native, sound by sound, word by word, expression by expression, and not attempt to go beyond this, till he has become so established in correct pronunciation, in his knowledge of the correct value of words and in the actual forms used by the Natives that there is no danger of his substituting something of his own for the real language.

It is by no means sufficient to learn a sound or expression once or ten times: it can only be correctly acquired by exercise, by thousands of repetitions, referring every time immediately to a correct standard. If a man reads for an hour with a teacher and then goes on attempting to pronounce the words by himself for the rest of the day, he will inevitably acquire a false pronunciation, unless he is so thoroughly established in a correct pronunciation that there is no danger of his losing it, and then indeed abundant exercise of his tongue, when alone, will be of the utmost use, but this at first is ruinous.

Suppose a child were shown the form of a letter and then as soon as he had a rough idea of it should go on writing repetitions of it without a standard before him, any body can tell what would be the consequence ; at the end of a month he would be thoroughly confirmed in writing such a letter as had never been seen before ; and if he had occasionally the standard put before him, the consequence would be that nine tenths of his time would be passed in learning to recede further from the original, and the other tenth in trying to get rid of the habit of writing wrong and to bring himself back to what was correct.

The same is the case with the student of languages, and in general they *are* thus constantly employed in partially learning and then unlearning, and the consequence is that even where an approach is made to a correct use of the language nine tenths of the time employed is needlessly lost.

A third point is to learn one thing at a time.

If a number of things are pressing upon the attention at once, it is impossible that a distinct and permanent impression can be received by any mind whatever its powers. Let us consider a person learning a language in the way so commonly followed. He is grappling with a sentence of many words. Here he has at once to consider, the character, the meaning of many new words, the pronunciation of them all, the inflexions of the nouns and verbs, the syntax, the mode of expression, &c. The consequence is, his attention is so overwhelmed and distracted that his mind is incapable of receiving a clear impression on any one point. No wonder that so little progress is made, that the knowledge acquired is so imperfect and incorrect, and that the student is so constantly discouraged. Often his progress is one continued effort to bear up against the most depressing feeling that he can never master the difficulties, as a man wears himself out sometimes in trying to carry a load beyond his strength, when if he would divide it and carry a portion of it at a time, he would not only accomplish his task and that comfortably, but would gain strength by the exercise. How many, especially in hot climates are so injured in their health, not by learning a language; but by the way in which they learn it, that when they have some use of it they are obliged to lay by for a time. Whereas if they would learn one thing at a time, they would attain to such a clear and sound knowledge and go on so comfortably that they would be in no danger of ending without an effective use of the language.

A fourth point is to take care to give the whole strength to the really essential parts of the subject. What are the things that constitute a sound knowledge in this case? Certainly not a loose imperfect idea of the value of almost all the words of the language, with a rough guess at their pronunciation and the mode of putting them together, the power of reading the character, of understanding a book with the help of time for consideration, of recognizing the words by *sight* &c. This is the foundation that is usually laid; such a student now commences to apply his knowledge of the language to the principal, perhaps the only purpose for which he has studied it; viz., conversation. He finds of course that his being able to recognize the words when he sees them is of no use to him; he has no facility in recognizing them by the ear, which was the only thing he required; he says the Native, he is attempting to talk with, speaks too fast. The fact is that he has not been learning the one grand thing he had to learn, the use of his ear. Next, he finds his knowing all the words in the language, in a certain way is of little or no use to him, because what he needs is the perfectly ready, familiar use of one in ten of them, but he cannot put a dozen together in that ready way which is necessary for conversing.

Next, when he has with much difficulty put a sentence together he is paralyzed by seeing a civil, enquiring stare on the countenance of his companion, in consequence of the imperfection of his pronunciation, and the English mode of expression he uses. His failure usually produces utter discouragement, unless he has such a good opinion of himself that he attributes it entirely to the stupidity of the Native. In reality he has been giving the whole of his attention to matters that are of little or no use to him, while he has almost entirely neglected those that are essential.

This brings us to the fifth principle, that *the language must be learnt by the ear and not by the eye.* This is one of the great fundamental mistakes made almost universally in studying living languages: the student never for a moment studies without seeing the words, though he knows that his whole object is to recognize them by his ear, without any assistance from the eye. A man might just as well attempt to train himself for a walking journey by sitting down for a year and turning a winch with his arms, or try to strengthen his limbs by moving for 6 months on crutches. Every body knows the consequence of this system, but every body pursues it. From the first the ear must be the main medium of receiving instruction and though the eye may be used a little at first with some advantage just to help the memory, yet after a little time the ear should be employed alone in conversation.

A man may consider he has laid a sound foundation when he has made the following acquisitions.

1st. The perfectly accurate pronunciation and thoroughly familiar knowledge of a certain number of the most generally used words, however small, so that they are to him exactly as words of his own language, that is, that he has not to search about in his memory for them when he wants them, but that they will come of themselves, and these pronounced so that a native cannot but recognize them.

2nd. The power of putting these together in a good number of real bonâ fide native expressions, however short, without any effort, expressions which he can confidently use, because he knows they are real, as he actually learnt them from a native, and not ones that he has invented and which consequently may or may not convey the meaning he intended or any meaning. One will often hear a native who has learnt English at a School use a sentence which is unexceptionable as to grammar &c., but which is objectionable as conveying no meaning whatever to an Englishman. Thus a Tamil man may say in English, "If you see this that's good," and the Englishman to whom it is addressed cannot even guess what he means to express, though the same expression conveys a clear idea to the Tamulian.

3rd. An ear so exercised in the sounds of the language that the words spoken by a native, if they have been learnt, are at once recognized by the student so that what is said within the limit of the student's vocabulary can be apprehended at once without seeing the words written, and without a moment's consideration.

4th. The knowledge of so much grammar as is necessary to form sentences of a few words only.

This is the sort of knowledge of a language that a child of three or four years old has. He doesn't know a single rule of grammar, he can't perhaps read or write a letter, his whole vocabulary probably consists of a thousand words, but within the limits of the matters he has to converse about, he can say with perfect freedom and almost perfect correctness any thing he wants without a moment's hesitation, and he understands on the instant every thing that's said to him, and that even though some of the words used are unknown to him. He has in fact a sound foundation, what he knows is real, and he has only to go on adding to his stock of words and expressions, and to correct some unimportant errors, which however are such as do not in the least prevent his being understood. An adult student, who has such a knowledge, is in a right position, because he can converse within certain limits, and therefore he is in the way of exercising himself *in contact* with a correct standard, and he has nothing of consequence to unlearn; his progress is not stopped by established habits of false pronunciation, and false expression, nor by habitual dependance upon his eyes to assist his memory. His only care then in conversation should be, not to attempt too much, but to content himself with common subjects and simple expressions, and only giving himself more liberty, as by learning he increases his stock of words, expressions &c. The knowledge of the character has nothing to do with this foundation, it is not in any way an assistance in acquiring it, and it is a great hindrance. A child uses his language freely and correctly without knowing a letter. *The character has no connection with the pronunciation of a language*, which must be learnt by the ear alone, and the sounds so acquired are just as well represented by the student's own letters as by any others. Neither is a knowledge of almost the whole language necessary to it, the words in common use about ordinary matters form only a very small proportion of the words of a language, and three fourths of the words which occur in the books ordinarily read are of no use whatever to the beginner; they are on the contrary the greatest hindrance to him by preventing his thoroughly learning those that he ought to have a familiar use of. Let us recapitulate the things necessary to form a sound foundation.

1st. A small vocabulary thoroughly known and become as familiar as the words of one's mother tongue.

2nd. An accurate pronunciation of these and the organs of speech thoroughly exercised in them, so that they can be spoken with perfect freedom.

3rd. So much grammar as is necessary to put these words together in short simple forms of expression.

4th. An ear so thoroughly exercised in the sounds of the commonest words as spoken by a native that they can be instantly recognized when *heard*.

5th. The knowledge of a considerable stock of the commonest expressions of the language, so that the words known can be made into bonâ fide sentences.

When such a foundation has been laid, the student has only to proceed to add more words, more grammar and more expressions by degrees, only taking care to learn nothing but what is immediately wanted and to learn thoroughly whatever is learnt at all. When considerable progress has thus been made, he may proceed to learn the character if he requires it and to read books &c.

Let us now consider more particularly the second main point, viz., To save time.

As in other matters, the right way of acquiring a correct knowledge of a language will be found to be suitable for the attainment of this main object also.

The things that are necessary to ensure a sound foundation are equally so to secure the saving of time; but we will now consider the details especially with reference to the latter. The first thing then is, to do one thing at a time. Surely this is a principle that will at once commend itself to every one. We have to learn the character, the words, pronunciation, the grammar, the expressions &c. Our plan therefore should be as far as possible to separate these, and have the attention concentrated upon one of them at a time. This certainly cannot be fully accomplished; but it can be sufficiently, for practical purposes.

The second is, to learn thoroughly whatever is learnt. How can there be any question about the waste of time produced by partially learning things and so forgetting them over and over again? We may safely say that, as ordinarily studied, the meaning of every word, its pronunciation, points of grammar, expressions &c., are partially learnt and forgotten again hundreds of times over. Everything that is learnt should be so followed up that it may be indelibly fixed in the memory and be as much part of the student himself as any thing in his own language.

3rd. Learn only what is really wanted. Surely this also is most obvious. To learn at first words which will either never be of any use to him, or not till he is far advanced in the language, is entire waste of time. The same with forms of expression &c.

An Englishman never thinks it necessary to learn all the words of his own language, he never knows half of them, much as he reads; and how many must there be in every language that he need never know. The student should first begin with such words as are of universal use in common life and then, when he has made some progress in the language, commence upon those which are necessary for his particular profession. Even in English there are numbers of words which, though common in books, are never used in ordinary conversation; but this is much more the case in languages in which ninety nine hundredths of the people scarcely ever read a book at all. To the beginner such book words, as he cannot distinguish them from others, are nothing but a serious hindrance to him.

Bishop Heber remarks that to make himself intelligible to the great mass of his hearers who were uneducated persons, he used to find it advisable to confine himself as far as possible to words of Saxon-derivation, that is, to words commonly used in conversation. If such a precaution were necessary in England, how much more in semi-civilized countries.

Can there be any question but that by a system of study based upon these principles, by far the largest part of the time usually spent upon acquiring a colloquial use of a foreign language may be saved. Look at the progress a child makes in a really useful knowledge of a language, whether his first, or one picked up afterwards, from being associated with those who speak it, with such extremely small powers of mind, without any effort, and without any materials. Can it be supposed that an adult with such enormous advantages, with properly prepared materials, and with diligent study could not make much more rapid progress, if he pursued a right system.

The system that I would now propose, founded on these principles, is as follows.

1st. The language is to be learnt through the medium of the English character.

The object of this is to get rid of any thing which is not absolutely necessary to be learnt at first.

It may be said that it takes a very little time to learn the native character; and so it does to learn it *in a certain way*, that is, so that by fixing the thoughts upon a letter and taking a little time for consideration, it may be recollected to represent a certain sound, but it will be a long time before the character is so familiar as not to occupy the attention most seriously, and that at the time when there is the greatest demand upon it. But not only is a known character preferable at first on this account, but it is also superior as a medium to the native character, as being less liable to lead to mistakes. In an Indian language for instance, in which there are two or three n's and as many l's, the beginner is always liable to forget which is which; but the plan of noting the sound by English letters with one or two dots under those that represent peculiar native sounds, effectually prevents any such mistakes, the dots remind the reader in the readiest manner that they represent such sounds as are those upon which the attention should be especially concentrated. Every letter in the native language must be represented by one certain letter of English, so that the proper spelling may be known. As to the learning of the native character ultimately, if the student should require it, its the easiest thing in the world when the language is known in other respects, and the whole attention is available for the letters only. The time required for this is most trifling but even were it considerable it would still be necessary to learn at first through the medium of the English character, on account of the enormous loss of time arising from having the attention overburthened at first. I therefore reject the native character as being

1st. Quite unnecessary for learning the language.

2nd. As being a most serious hindrance, absorbing a great deal of the attention, when its utmost efforts are required for those things which are essential.

3rd. As not being required at all by a great proportion of those who need to acquire a foreign language.

4th. As a thing that can be acquired with a hundredth part of the time which would be consumed at first, after the other parts of the study have been matured.

5th. As being more liable to be mistaken by the beginner than the English character.

If it be said, but how can it be avoided when there are no elementary books of the language in the English character? I answer,

First, that I am here proposing a new system, and of course would have books prepared suitable to it; Second, that in many languages, as in those of Bengal, many books have already been prepared in this way; Third, that in many situations the student could, with the assistance of a native, easily provide himself with the first elementary books, without much loss of time, and certainly with much less expenditure of time, than by studying in the common ways with such books as are already provided; and Fourthly, that if there is no alternative, we must of course begin by learning the native character, but still if we follow out the other parts of the system here proposed, it will be much less a hindrance to him than to those who adopt the usual means, because he will seldom have to read any words but those which he knows, and then the strange character is comparatively a small hindrance. Of course, in applying the English character, the value of each letter must first be defined, as is now fully recognized as an essential principle, and which is always acted upon in the Bengal books. The letter, A, for instance, has in English seven distinct sounds as in the words, hat, mast, all, many, America, Yacht, make. In all the East Indian languages, the letter which represents the sound of our A, in Mast or long A, somewhat modified, represents the sound of our A in amuse, or short A, and therefore this letter, with and without a long mark over it, should represent these two sounds and be used whenever the corresponding characters are used or implied in the foreign word. With respect to the other sounds of it, some are unknown in certain languages, as for instance the sounds of that letter in the words hat and Yacht are unknown in any Asiatic language. No Native Indian can pronounce the words hat and hot, but are under the necessity of substituting some other vocal sound for them, till they have learnt the true pronunciation. The other sounds of it will of course be represented by those English vowels which more properly represent them, only taking care, to use the same letter to represent the long and short sound, distinguishing the former by a long mark over it. Thus the sound of E in Hen, and Féte, which are properly the same sound pronounced long or short, are represented in the Indian languages by modifications of the same letter and should therefore both be represented by E. With respect to the sounds which are either unknown in English, or not represented by any one English letter, they should either be represented by a combination of English letters, if possible, or if not by a letter or letters, distinguished by a mark; as for instance one or more dots under them. There are, for instance, four letters that represent in the Tamil language the sound of our N, or some modification of it; one, is precisely the sound of it, the tongue being placed in the same position as by us. This will be represented of course by our N. The second is the same in sound, though represented by a different character, but it occurs only when preceding and combined with a certain other consonant, this may also be represented by a simple English N, as the sound is the same. The third has the sound of Ny in English and therefore should be represented by those consonants, the sound is that of our N, in "New." The fourth is a sound unknown in English: it is pronounced by the tongue being turned entirely back, so that the under part of its tip touches the roof of the mouth. An N, sounded with the tongue in this position is the sound required. This therefore should be represented by an N, with a dot under it, the dot or dots being the invariable mark of a sound quite strange to an Englishman, so as to be the readiest warning to the student that the tongue must be placed in a position which is new to him. This is much preferable to the native character itself, because there can be no mistake about it without any effort of memory, whereas the foreign character will always require the student to consider which of the several sounds of N it represents.

It may be observed here, that, in general, probably in all cases, the languages of semi-civilized people that are written, have an invariable sound for each character, so that there is no such difficulty in representing them by the English characters as there would be in representing English by some foreign character, on account of the vocal sounds being represented in different words by different vowels; as, Hat, yacht, many, all &c., and grief, leaf, seed, previous, Marine, receive, and homœopathy. In writing English therefore in a foreign character, there would be no alternative but to use a certain letter for each sound, however that sound is represented in English writing, and correct English spelling must be learnt afterwards. But these difficulties do not exist in applying the English character to represent the sounds of most of the written languages of semi-civilized nations.

2nd. Begin with a restricted vocabulary. In the first place, reject of course all words which will never be required, such as those used only in learned works: next, reject all those that hardly ever occur even in books. Next let alone those that are chiefly in use only in certain particular lines of life, and are more or less technical. Again, have nothing to do with any words that are not commonly used in the ordinary matters of life. What can be gained but clear loss by burthening the young beginner with a multitude of words, by far the greater part of those in the language, that will be thus rejected, when they have nothing whatever to do with his acquiring a useful knowledge of the language, and when, if required, they can afterwards be added in a tenth part of the time that they would require at first. Probably out of twenty thousand words in a language, the knowledge of 5000 would set him so perfectly at liberty in all ordinary conversation that neither he himself nor those he converses with would be reminded that he does not know all. And if occasionally a person used one of the remaining words, probably he could not mistake the meaning of it in the midst of so many known ones. And if he could not perceive what it must mean, he could have no difficulty in asking the meaning or understanding the explanation. Having thus relieved our student from such a mass of useless labour, let us next divide these 5000 words, or whatever the number is, into several portions, taking out first one thousand and then another of the least common and least immediately necessary words, till we have only a thousand left. Out of these we again take 250 three times, and then 150 in the same way, so that to begin we have only 100 of the commonest words in the language, but consisting of all the different parts of speech so that little sentences may be formed out of them. The learner then deals with only one of these batches of words at a time, not troubling himself with the others till he knows the first batch as well as he does so many words of his own language. This is one of the great essentials of the system proposed. Words should never be partially learnt and forgotten again, nor imperfectly, that is, so that their true value and use are not thoroughly known. When once a word is taken up, it should of course be thoroughly secured both as respects the meaning of it and its use, and it must be particularly observed that it is not the bare knowledge of a word that is wanted, so that a person by more or less thought can recall it to his mind, it must, to be of any use in conversation, be perfectly familiar, and it must have been repeated aloud so many times that the organs of speech have been thoroughly exercised in it, and that it may be pronounced both correctly and with the utmost freedom. Nothing but *multiplied repetitions of it aloud with continued reference to a correct standard, and in connection with various other words can accomplish this.* It must take some time thus to appropriate new words, and especially the first 100 words of a language, but the process cannot possibly be hastened, but on the contrary indefinitely delayed, by attempting thousands of others before the first are secured.

The number 100 is chosen for the first batch, as being about the smallest number that can enable one to make up some variety of short sentences, so that each word may be seen in a variety of situations and in its various inflections ; and they are sufficient to provide for exercising the student in the first rudiments of grammar.

3rd. To each of these batches of words a set of sentences is to be added ; these are all to be the commonest colloquial expressions. They should consist of a certain number written on each word in the batch, and contain no words that are not in it. It is essential that they should be written by Natives, and those who cannot speak English would be preferable, in order that there may be a security for the sentences being true Native expressions. It is also essential that the writers should not be highly educated men, but ordinary intelligent men of the middle classes, otherwise the sentences would be almost sure to be full of fanciful things. The list of words should be given to several different persons in order to secure a good variety of expressions, and some selection should be made. The first set ought not to consist of less than 1000 sentences, that is 10 to each word, in order that by means of this batch of words the first rudiments of grammar may be quite familiar, and some considerable notion obtained of the general style of expression peculiar to the language, keeping throughout the grand object in view, which is to arrange that, so far as possible, the attention may be concentrated on one thing at a time. When a hundred words have been acquired, all the use possible should be made of them as the vehicle for conveying instructions in other respects before the attention is encumbered by new words, in order that when new words *are* taken in hand the student may have his attention in a great measure released from the pressure of the elementary points of grammar, peculiar style of expression &c.

It is also most essential that these sentences should consist of only two or three words, never more than the latter. It is astonishing how very little new matter overloads the attention of a beginner, and the utmost care is necessary that no more should ever be placed before him at a time than that he can receive a distinct impression of it. A sentence of four or five words is quite too much at first, and nothing is gained by attempting more than the student is equal to. Comparatively speaking, a very considerable time must be given to the first set of sentences, for there is a great deal to be learnt by them.

It is evident that they involve almost all the pronunciation, the inflexions of the nouns and verbs, the mode of combining the different parts of speech, the exercise of the organs of speech and that of the ear on the sound of the language &c.

The first progress of a student in a new language, at least in one entirely dissimilar to his native tongue, is indeed astonishingly slow, and it is of no use attempting to push him on faster than he can go. We constantly meet with what are called, easy books for beginners, but probably there is not one published in any language that is a hundredth part easy enough or that does not seem to suppose a progress at first a hundred times more rapid than any student makes.

The sentences must of course be translated into English, but it is essential that they should not be written originally in English and then translated into the foreign language.

We do not want to teach a man to speak English sentences in foreign words, but to use the foreign expressions.

The second set of words consisting of 150 may perhaps contain ten sentences for each word, or 1,500 in all.

These may be a little longer than the first, as the student will be able to obtain a clear impression of a greater number of words together, but probably they should not exceed five. After this, the sets of sentences may consist of fewer upon each word, and perhaps only one upon each of the last two batches, and they may be lengthened gradually, the last being of any length.

The essential points of these sentences are therefore,

First, that they should be bonâ fide expressions commonly used in the language, and consequently that they should be originally written in the language by a native.

2nd, That they should be simple, ordinary, colloquial expressions, and therefore that they should not be written by learned men who would probably spoil them. 3rd, That they should be extremely short, the first set not exceeding three words, and the others very gradually lengthened. 4th, That there should be a large number of them in the first set of words, so as to make as much use as possible of those words before proceeding to new ones. 5th, That there should be as great a variety of expressions in the sentences as possible.

In printing the sentences there should be, first, the native words separately and in the proper character: 2nd, Under each of them the same word in the English character: 3rd, The most exact English meaning of each individual word; and 4th, The full power of the sentence freely given in English.

The use of the Native character is, to enable a native to teach from the book, who does not know English.

As one great point in preparing these materials is, to provide for a person having to learn the language, with the help of natives who do not understand English, or who are not thoroughly qualified teachers, it is desirable if possible that these sentences should have numerous notes subjoined, giving all the information that can be suggested by each sentence and that can in any way help to give the student an intelligent knowledge of the language. These notes should if possible be written by an intelligent Englishman, who will know from his own experience what misapprehensions beginners are liable to form on account of their English ideas, and what points are likely to be difficulties to them. If the first two sets of words had ten sentences in each, and the last thousand words four on each, the whole of the sentences, on, suppose, 2,000 words would amount, to about 10,000, which would be sufficient to make the student thoroughly at home in expressing himself freely on all common subjects. Besides these general words and sentences, each student, according to his profession, ought to have a separate set of words and expressions belonging to his peculiar occupations, whether those of a Magistrate, a Merchant, a Missionary, an Engineer, &c.

But it would be of no use his acquiring this information till he was in some good measure grounded in the more general use of the language, and therefore he should not perhaps take such a list of words in hand till he had gone through the first two thousand general words with their sentences. The professional sentences should contain, of course, only those words already learnt in addition to the technical words. With these sets of words and sentences there should be a short grammar, containing only the first rudiments, in the simplest possible form, so that it can be referred to without loss of time on any point. This however in fact should be made comparatively very little use of. Rules of grammar are not wanted, a man in conversation cannot possibly stop to form the participle of a verb from the root, by considering the rules. If it does not come of itself into his mouth nothing can make amends for that defect. What is wanted is, such a knowledge of grammar as a child of four years old possesses ; that is, a knowledge which enables him to speak correctly, intelligibly, and without hesitation, though he does not know a single rule for anything he says. His speaking *must* be independent of any rules, whether he has learnt any or not. Yet a short grammar, to be looked into occasionally, at first may be of some little assistance in acquiring the inflexions of the nouns and verbs, &c. But the grand means of acquiring a grammatical use of the language must be simply the repetition multiplied, of a good variety of correct forms of expression.

Nothing can be more absurd than insisting upon knowing the rules of grammar before a student can be allowed to know a language.

If a man talks English grammatically, that is, correctly, he is never examined as to whether he knows any rules ; perhaps he never learnt a line of any English grammar, but it makes no difference. But it is always expected that a man studying a foreign language should be able to stand an examination of a kind neither he nor his examiner could stand in his mother tongue. The same man who meets a stranger in the street and knows well by the first sentence that he utters whether he is perfectly acquainted with English or not, is perhaps on his way to some place where he will pass hours in ascertaining whether a student has a good knowledge of a language foreign to him.

These are therefore the materials which I would put into any man's hands, who wants to study a foreign language for colloquial purposes: viz., a vocabulary of perhaps 2,000 words, divided into sets of, from 100 to 250, with about ten thousand common forms of expression, composed only of each set of words and those words previously learnt. These printed both in the Native and English character, with a verbal and a free translation, the sentences to be aided if possible by copious notes giving all the collateral information possible ; and to these to be added a very short rudimental grammar.

It will not perhaps be necessary to give the verbal translations of any but the first 2 or 3000 sentences.

As to the student's further study, he may of course now with perfect ease follow the ordinary plan; that is, take up any book that contains the sort of words and matter most suited to his line of life, with an ordinary dictionary and grammar to which however he will have very seldom to refer. He will know so large a proportion of the words that the context will generally shew the meaning of any new word he meets with, and he will lose very little of his time in that which usually occupies about three fourths of all the time expended in such studies, viz. in turning over the leaves of a large dictionary and guessing which of the several meanings there found for a word is compatible with those of the other words of the sentence before him, many of which he has also yet to ascertain. But his great business should of course be to converse as constantly as possible in order further to exercise his tongue and his ear, and to add to his stock of forms of expression. It is to be remembered that, in using books, a principal exercise should be, reading aloud and having them read aloud to him by a native.

If his occupation will require formal writing or translating, of course he must exercise himself a good deal with books. It is well known that the most easy and certain way of acquiring a correct and easy style in writing in any foreign language is to make or procure accurate translations of native books, and then retranslate them, comparing such re-translation with the original and thoroughly considering the difference between them. This can be done with the greatest ease and economy of time when such a good fundamental knowledge has been acquired as is supposed to be obtained through the system now proposed.

The next point to be considered is the mode of using these materials.

The student begins with the English letters representing the sounds. The teacher sounds each letter and the student repeats it immediately after. This is done many times with those letters which represent sounds entirely strange to the learner. The most essential thing is to learn where to place the tongue in these last sounds, without doing which it is impossible he should utter them correctly; and this must be most patiently and diligently practised, because this new motion of the tongue must be acquired to the same degree of facility as he has in pronouncing the sounds of his own langnage. This cannot possibly be effected except by long continued use of the organs of speech. At first, each of these letters should be pronounced perhaps ten times over by the teacher, and repeated by the student instantly, the latter always observing carefully the difference between his own pronunciation and that of the teacher's, which immediately follows.

The grand means to attain to a correct pronunciation must always be thus for the learner to attempt it both immediately after, and immediately before, hearing it correctly pronounced by a native. Just as in learning to write it is not sufficient first to look at the original and then try to imitate it, but after writing it to look again at the original to see in what respect the copy has failed. Of course it will only be necessary to do this with the new sounds, which will generally be only very few.

The student next takes the first list of 100 words, which are all written in the shortest form, that is, the radical form of the verb &c., as we should write in English, good, go, little, come, &c. The teacher should then pronounce the first word deliberately and distinctly and the student should repeat it, followed by the English meaning of it, when it should again be repeated by the teacher, and this suppose five times at first.

In this way the whole hundred words would be gone over many hundred times before the student ventures to attempt pronouncing them by himself. The teacher and student should sit at some distance apart, so that it may be necessary to speak pretty loud. In these first exercises the student should have the printed words before him, that he may have the assistance of sight in addition to that of hearing in impressing them on his memory. It will of course be at first tiresome to continue this exercise long, nevertheless the longer the better, and if a person could arrange to do it for one or two hours, at three or four different times in the day it would probably be best—but he should not attempt to learn them by heart because his pronunciation will not be sufficiently confirmed.

When he has become tolerably familiar with the words of the first set of sentences, both as to pronunciation and meaning, by thus repeating them with his teacher several times and with his book before him, he should put down his book and go over them again in the same way several times, without seeing the words, so as to be wholly dependent upon the ear. From the first, the ear must be exercised as far as possible without any aid from the eye. It must be kept continually in mind that the sight is to be used as little as possible for the reasons before given. The sentence should not be read together the first time of going over because the student is not yet able to receive any distinct impression from more than one word at a time. The student should not yet trouble himself about the mode of framing the inflexions that he meets with, but be content to take the word with its exact English meaning as he finds it. In this way he should go through the first 1,000 sentences with his teacher which will perhaps take him 15 hours, or suppose three days study, during which time he would have repeated every one of the first hundred words on an average about a hundred and fifty times (including the separate readings of the list of words).

Less than three times repetition of each word is not sufficient to ensure the students correcting himself when he pronounces it imperfectly the first time.

After the first and second reading of the sentences, repeating each word by word, the whole sentence should be repeated in the same way at least three times over, the student repeating the free English translation after the foreign sentence.

The readings should be repeated till every word has been heard and uttered suppose 600 times. During these readings the grammar of the nouns and verbs may be looked into a little; and, lastly, the sentence should be learnt by heart. And when the student is well exercised in the pronunciation by these means, so that he can trust himself to utter it without first hearing it spoken, the sentence should be again gone over in the same way, but the teacher beginning by repeating first the English word, when the student gives the foreign one, the teacher immediately repeating it again and so on. But if it is found that the student cannot yet remember the word and pronounce it with perfect ease, they should be read over again in the former way. When able to do it, the whole set of sentences should be again gone through without the words being repeated individually, the teacher the first time giving the foreign sentence, and the next time giving first the English sentence.

It may be supposed that all this will not be necessary; and it certainly is not, in order to obtain such a knowledge as is usually supposed to be sufficient, that is, a knowledge which, when brought to the trial of conversation, is found to be of little or no use. But it will be found that, to obtain a really familiar acquaintance with this first set of words and their easy and correct pronunciation and use, these multiplied repetitions are absolutely necessary.

Nothing but a long continued exercise of the ear and the organs of speech upon a great variety of actual expressions can give either that quickness at hearing and pronouncing, or that facility of correctly combining the words, which are essential to their effective colloquial use.

It must be particularly observed that this first set of sentences thus acquired implies much more than might appear from the first glance, namely, there is involved in it as it were the whole pronunciation of the language; for a man who can pronounce freely and correctly 100 words will have little difficulty in pronouncing all the rest: 2nd, a knowledge of all the inflexions of the nouns and verbs: 3rd, the mode of combining and arranging the different parts of speech.

Thus, though only 100 words are used, some real and considerable progress has already been made in the knowledge of the language.

This first set of sentences should not be laid aside till they are so perfectly familiar, that almost any one of them can be repeated with the utmost readiness, on the English translation being uttered. Nothing whatever will be gained by meddling with new materials till these first are thoroughly wrought into the student, and made as much part of himself as the words and expressions of his own language.

The second set of words and sentences must be read over and thoroughly appropriated in the same way as the first.

Probably these first 250 words with their sentences may be mastered in a month of steady study of 3 or 4 hours a day, and 750 additional words with about 3000 longer sentences in another month, completing the first 1000 words in two months. After the thorough grounding which this will give in every respect, in pronunciation, in expression, in hearing, in grammar &c. the additions will be made with much greater rapidity.

Every thing depends upon this first grounding being thorough and complete. Nothing but such repetitions will accomplish this object—there is no other way of doing it.

A soldier may be shewn how to march, and he may be made to move his legs in the manner shewn in a few steps, but nothing but long continued practise can possibly enable him to do it both correctly and with ease; and it is the same with the muscles of the tongue, the ear, and the brain, as it is with the limbs.

A girl may have the finest ear possible, but that will not enable her fingers to run over the notes of a piano or her throat to produce the notes of a song freely and correctly, without long exercise of those organs.

After the first month the teacher will be required much less, because the student can be trusted to pronounce when he is alone, provided he exercises with the teacher for some time daily. He should always read aloud by himself just as when he reads with the teacher, both because, the great point is the exercise of the organs of speech, and hearing, and also because the pronouncing of the word is so great a help to remember the meaning. It must however be remembered that in this solitary study as little use as possible should still be made of the eye. The word or sentence should be merely glanced at when necessary and the repetition should then be made without looking at the book.

With respect to the time required, I cannot speak certainly, because I have never had an opportunity of seeing the study commenced with such materials properly prepared beforehand; but so far as I have seen it tried with imperfect materials, the result was certainly excellent.

In the only case where an approach was made to a fair trial, a gentleman studied irregularly, but equal to about two months continuous study of five hours a day, and from that time he went out and performed all his duties without an interpreter, having constantly to converse with the middling and lower classes, most of whom had never spoken to a European before.

This was a real, practical and effective acquaintance with the language, though within small limits as to his number of words and expressions at first starting; but then his ear and tongue having been well exercised, he could both make himself understood and he could recognize the words spoken to him, and consequently he was in a position to make steady progress in the correct use of the language from his intercourse with the people, and this he accordingly did. It would of course have been much better if he could have continued the same course of study, though it were only for an hour or two a day, by which he would have far more rapidly added to his stock of words and expressions.*

It is very probable that many persons would complete the appropriation of the first 1,000 words and their sentences in one month.

I would now only ask which is preferable as a foundation, such a really effective use of a language, though within small limits; or such a loose, vague, and useless knowledge of a vast number of

* An educated Native, who had, I believe, helped to teach this gentleman, lately told me that he had overheard Natives speaking of him, who said that if they had not seen him, they should not have known that it was not a Native who was speaking Teloogoo.

words, with the rules of grammar, as is usually acquired after at least many months of hard study, during the whole of which time too, the attention has been kept in a very injurious state of tension by the overwhelming load of new things that has continually been laid upon it at one and the same time. I believe that in general little effective colloquial use of such a language is acquired within a year of hard study, and that often two or three years or more pass before the student can talk it tolerably, though only a portion of that time of course is actually employed in study. On one occasion, I was acquainted with two men who studied intensely (about ten hours a day) for nine months, after which upon trial they found that they could scarcely hold the slightest communication with natives.

A remarkably apposite passage from the life of Dr. Hope may here be quoted which I have just met with, and in which a part of the very means here proposed is stated to have been used by him with the most remarkable success, though he did not begin upon this plan, but merely learnt the colloquial use of a language after he had acquired a considerable stock of words. " He had already picked up a good knowledge of French and Italian, so far as mere reading went, and he imagined like many others that a little practice on the road would enable him to speak the language sufficiently to carry him through his tour; but it was a very different thing to hear the lessons of professors and to converse with the natives of the country. Of this he found a very humiliating proof. He went to engage apartments at a private Hotel, but after a pantomimic performance of twenty minutes between himself and the landlady, it was found that neither could in the slightest degree understand the other, and after laughter and reciprocal bows he returned in despair. Having settled at another hotel, he now determined to devote twelve hours a day to the mere practice of speaking French. His first step was to engage a French Master for twelve lessons and to make him go through the drudgery of reading three words at a time, while he mimicked them as closely as he could. This was singularly disagreeable to the master, but it was all that Dr. Hope wanted and he was inflexible. He thus secured himself against any gross error in pronunciation. He happened to possess a Wanostrocht's grammar with a key to it, a grammar which is remarkable for the *great number* of *simple exercises* which illustrate each rule.

He now translated these exercises from English to French, correcting himself by constant reference to the Key. In this way he went two or three times through the grammar in the course of a month, *gaining flexibility of tongue* and losing the fear of hearing his own voice. He at the same time adopted another device; he went to dine daily at a small and crowded restaurant frequented by the Garde du corps, where the company was so closely packed that he could not help hearing the conversation of two or three contiguous talkers. In this way his ear got *familiarized with all the sounds of the French language,* whether quick or slow, correct or provincial. At the end of a month he ventured to sally forth, and, having a fancy for the rooms of the private hotel to which he had originally gone, he waited on the landlady. On entering he addressed her in fluent French, explained his wishes &c., the landlady the meanwhile, with up-raised hands and a look of utter amazement, exclaiming, "Voilâ un miracle! you cannot be the same gentleman that called here a month ago and could not speak a word of French."

This case has no reference to the principles here proposed, so far as the use of a restricted vocabulary is concerned, but it shews how perfectly ineffectual the knowledge of book language and the exercise of the eye was, for colloquial purposes, and how complete the success was both in respect of time and effect, when the means here proposed were used, viz., the thorough appropriation of a good stock of simple familiar sentences, and the diligent exercise of the ear and tongue.

He was totally without the colloquial use of the language, so that he could neither understand a word spoken nor speak one intelligibly when he began to adopt the means he did, and in one month he found himself perfectly at liberty in conversation.

In the same memoir it is afterwards related;—"Having had a lesson in France on the inconvenience of not being able to speak the language of a country in which one is travelling and studying, Dr. Hope guarded against a similar inconvenience in Italy.

Before leaving Paris he improved his pronunciation of Italian by taking twelve lessons, as he had formerly done in French, and he provided himself with a brief practical Italian Grammar, with Exercises referring to the rules, and a key to them.

During a tour in Switzerland it was agreed that he should walk in advance of his friend for an hour daily, to give him an opportunity of *practising these exercises viva voce.*

This plan answered perfectly; at the end of the time he spoke Italian fluently."

It may perhaps help to show yet more distinctly how far the principles here advocated differ from or agree with some of the commonly received notions on the subject, if I place my views side by side with those lately advanced in an elementary book for helping the student of an Indian language.

The 1st principle laid down is, "Don't proceed too quickly. An entirely new language requires great accuracy in the mastering of its elements." In this I agree, but I consider the book itself implies a progress in the learner immeasureably beyond the reality.

2nd, "Write down every thing from the beginning. Read always with pen or pencil in hand." This is directly opposed to two of my principles, one an essential one, the other, one of great importance. The first, that every thing is to be learnt through the ear, and not through the eye, because it is the ear that is to be employed in using the language and not the eye. The other, that the foreign character should not be used by the beginner, because time must be saved in learning one thing at a time, and the character is not necessary to enable one to learn the language itself.

3rd, "Read aloud all the exercises with a Tamil teacher, and be very careful in ascertaining the correctness of what you have written." Here it is evident that there was some sort of loose notion about the exercise of the *tongue*, but it also shows that there was nothing like a real apprehension of the essential importance of this, nor of the extent to which that exercise should be carried. Nor is any thing at all said about that which I insist upon, as the main point, viz., the impossibility of learning to pronounce correctly, and the certainty of being established in a false pronunciation, unless for some considerable time, no word is pronounced without referring at the time to a correct standard, without the student hearing one word at a time pronounced both immediately before and immediately after himself by a native. As to the latter clause of this hint I urge that the only possible way to secure the correctness of what one learns is not to attempt to invent anything, but to be content to learn every thing, every sound, every word, every expression from a native.

4th, "At first, whenever you meet with a new word, look for it in the vocabulary, and decline and conjugate it in full." My rule is, never meet with a new word, and never lose a minute in looking for a word in a vocabulary, or in *guessing* which of the different meanings that may be there given is the right one; and never lose time in declining and conjugating a word in full. Use only limited lists of words, and thoroughly appropriate every one by hearing it applied in a great variety of short sentences, in the course of which exercises, the grammar will necessarily be picked up long before the pronunciation and value and use of the word are fully acquired. Yet it will be of some use to look occasionally into a short grammar containing the inflexions of words.

5th, "Begin to talk, though with stammering lips, as soon as possible, the very first day. Never speak English to a native if you can help it. Why say salt, when you know the word, Uppu? Do not be afraid of making mistakes."

This rule contains the very essence of the ordinary system, or rather of the old notions. It is diametrically opposed to the universally acknowledged and universally applicable principle. "Whatever is habitual is easy." It is always easier to do a thing the second time than the first. My principle is, Be afraid of one thing, making mistakes. Every time that a mistake is made, one step more is taken towards a confirmed habit of making that mistake. Why do men in talking English as their own language go on putting h's in the wrong places and leaving them out all their lives, in spite of their getting into a different class of society, where they continually hear the correct pronunciation in this respect, without ever being corrected? Because by habit their perceptions have been so blunted that they never perceive that they make a mistake. Do we not keep this principle of avoiding mistakes in view in almost all other cases excepting this? Do we set a child to make a rude imitation of some letter and then leave him to repeat it without a standard? or, do we insist upon his incessantly looking at a standard, and never making one written letter without trying to imitate that standard which is placed before his eyes?

My principle therefore is, never attempt to guess at any thing, whether it is a sound, or word, or an expression. Take the most effective steps you can to prevent your ever "making a mistake." Is there not enough work to do to learn the real language, that you must take measures to oblige yourself to add to it the unlearning of your own mistakes? Every time you pronounce a word wrong you have that to unlearn. On no account therefore attempt to *speak* in the proper sense of that word till you are established in

1st. A sound pronunciation.
2nd. In the knowledge of the true value of a stock of words.
3rd. In that of a good amount of Grammar.
4th. In that of a large stock of bonâ fide native expressions.

Is not this principle undeniable? Does a drawing master tell his pupil, Go and make rude and absurd drawings of a hand or a foot, and then occupy yourself in unlearning the habit you have been acquiring, or does he set before his pupil a true representative of a thing, and say, Imitate this, with the most earnest and close attention and never make a line without referring to the standard? Which pupil would make the greatest progress and which would be most likely to attain to perfection in his study,— one who was always trying to make rude drawings of a foot out of his own imagination and then labouring to correct them, or one who did not attempt to invent at all, but kept exercising himself in imitating a correct representation of a foot.

6th, "Be very careful in noting down differences in idiom between your own language and Tamil. If you hear much Christian or Cutcherry Tamil, beware of thinking all you hear to be really Tamil. Try to cultivate a Tamil ear, so as to detect an unidiomatic expression as you would a false note in music. You should *understand* all you hear; you need not *use* any expression that is not good Tamil."

I would only ask how a student can possibly learn to distinguish between true language and false, except by learning the true, and taking care as far as possible not to come in contact with false language, whether coming from himself or any body else, till he has acquired a sound taste and judgment, by a *confirmed* knowledge of the true language.

The simple rule is, *Learn* the true language, and then you will not waste your time in acquiring and trying to unlearn a false one. Sow clean wheat in your ground, and not wheat and weeds mixed together, and then you will not require to employ all the season in trying in vain to root out the weeds which you have yourself sown.

It is this sort of instructions, continually inserted in books of instruction in languages, and which are directly opposed to well known general principles, which shew so plainly how entirely undigested the subject still is, and how people in general are still acting upon notions that they have never examined, and which will not bear the least examination.

In the book which is prefaced by these rules, the materials provided to assist the learner of Tamil are all prepared upon the usual false principles :—

1st. An unlimited vocabulary is used, so that every word must be learnt and forgotten a hundred times over.

2nd. All sorts of words are introduced, words perfectly useless to a beginner, words derived from Sanscrit and scarcely ever used in conversation, words used only in books translated from English by Englishmen &c.

3rd. The sentences are certainly not all written by a native, so that the learner takes up the book with the encouraging feeling that he does not know which are true Tamil sentences and which are not.

4th. Almost all the sentences are much too long for a beginner.

5th. Many of the sentences are such as it is quite useless for a beginner to learn.

6th. English sentences are given without the corresponding Tamil. How is the *learner* to discover what the proper Tamil would be unless he is told ?

7th. The same with the Tamil sentences. What can be the

use of leaving the *learner* to guess what the English meaning is, knowing that when he has guessed it, it may be either right or wrong. Suppose a Tamil man were learning English, how could he find out the expression we use when we ask who a certain person is? How could he ever guess the expression, Who's that? Or could he find out of himself these expressions, What's the matter? Where has he been? Come away. I'd rather not. Never mind. Whether or no. I can't help it. You might as well set a man to guess, at the words of a language as at its common expressions.

When I put this book into a Moonshee's hand, the first thing he said, was, Many of these sentences are not common Tamil expressions, and many of the words are not commonly used in conversation.

This might be said of almost any book, I suppose every book, of the kind. What is a learner to do who has no better materials? It is destructive for a learner to use a book, when he is not sure whether the sentences are Tamil or not.

I mention these particulars of this book, as illustrative of the mistakes, and undigested ideas that are current on the subject.

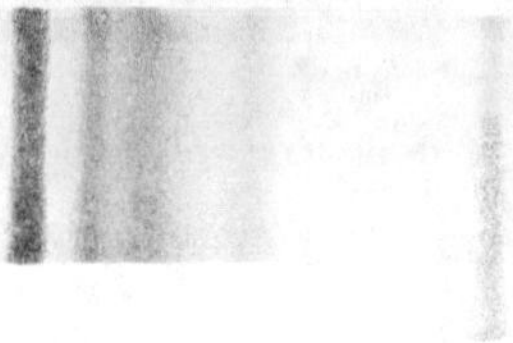